I0096754

GIVING HOUSING SUPPLY A BOOST

Giving Housing Supply A Boost
How to Improve Affordability and Reduce Homelessness

by Steven Greenhut and Wayne Winegarden

January 2024

ISBN: 978-1-934276-54-9

Pacific Research Institute
P.O. Box 60485
Pasadena, CA 91116

www.pacificresearch.org

Nothing contained in this report is to be construed as necessarily reflecting the views of the Pacific Research Institute or as an attempt to thwart or aid the passage of any legislation. The views expressed remain solely the authors'. They are not endorsed by any of the authors' past or present affiliations.

©2024 Pacific Research Institute. All rights reserved. No part of this publication may be reproduced, stored in a retrieval system, or transmitted in any form or by any means, electronic, mechanical, photocopy, recording, or otherwise, without prior written consent of the publisher.

GIVING HOUSING SUPPLY A BOOST
HOW TO IMPROVE AFFORDABILITY
AND REDUCE HOMELESSNESS

By Steven Greenhut and Wayne Winegarden

VOLUME FIVE

PR PACIFIC
RESEARCH
INSTITUTE

When Did California Housing Become So Pricey?

The roots of California's housing problems aren't particularly hard to trace given the reams of house-price and population data going back decades. For instance, the *Los Angeles Times* reported that the median price of a California home in 1970 was only 5% higher than the national average at $24,300.[1] That year's nationwide median price was $23,400, which translates to a low $181,000 price in 2023 dollars after adjusting for inflation.

In the same year that Richard Nixon was president, Apollo 13 circled the moon and the Beatles broke up, the median price in San Francisco was somewhat high at $28,000,[2] but that translates into a mere $227,000 today. That amount might buy a typical home in Louisville, Ky., but won't make much of a dent even as a down payment in the City by the Bay – despite falling prices driven by post-COVID population losses. The median San Francisco house now costs $1.4 million.[3]

It's a similar story throughout California and the West. In economically struggling Bakersfield, a dusty Central Valley industrial city far from the idyllic coast, the median price is $378,000.

In Wenatchee, Wash., a humble city in an agricultural region east of the Cascades, the median price is $490,000. Boise was named the least-affordable housing market recently given its low income levels and high prices. Prices there soared to a median of $550,000 in summer of 2022.[4]

Although this book focuses on California, other Western states have faced similar problems – and embraced similar housing policies – as California, at least in the last decade. When population soared, builders were unable to meet the new demand (often from refugees from pricey California coastal cities) and prices went upward. This reduced opportunities for local residents and bred hostility toward the newcomers, with Boise serving as a case in point.

A 2019 *Los Angeles Times* article was headlined: "'Go back to California': Wave of newcomers fuels backlash in Boise."[5] The sentiment even fueled a mayoral run by a candidate who jokingly proposed building a $26-billion wall to keep Californians from relocating there. But behind the anger (and the dark humor) was a simple numbers problem. As the article noted, wages in the area are low. Home prices soared by 19% or more a year. Rental vacancies became non-existent, leaving lower-income Boise-area residents with no place to move.

The people moving in generally had equity from their California home sales and typically had remote jobs or were retirees, so they weren't dependent on local wages. "Boise needs 1,000 new housing units each year for the next decade, according to officials in this city of 228,000," reported the *Times*. "That's just not happening."[6] Boise became a microcosm for the housing crisis that started along the California coast and made its way inland and even into the intermountain West.

So what happened? It's basic supply and demand. Government policies since the 1970s artificially constrained the supply of housing through slow-growth rules, urban-growth boundaries, an increase in developer fees, environmental laws and regulatory edicts including inclusionary zoning – i.e., requiring builders to set aside a percentage of under-market units in each project. Until recently, those cities' populations grew and the result is a disaster. Even Boise has its share of slow-growth regulations.[7]

California's nonpartisan Legislative Analyst's Office produced a noteworthy – and often quoted – 2015 report that provides historical context for the state's housing woes.[8] Since its publication, the pricing situation has gotten worse even as the Legislature has begun to roll back – albeit in a limited fashion – some of the rules that have led to the supply and demand imbalance. The LAO also points to 1970 as a pivotal year, noting that housing in the following decade soared from somewhat above the national average to 80% above it. Something changed in that decade – mostly a convergence of state and political forces that limited construction. The report said that California was underbuilding new housing by about 110,000 units a year, especially along the coast.[9]

We often hear from coastal city residents who, in arguing against new housing projects, note that not everyone has a right to live in an idyllic beachside community. They are right to a degree. One would always expect cities such as Santa Barbara, Santa

Cruz, Laguna Beach and La Jolla – with their perfect climate and magnificent views – to have higher prices than less-sought-after communities.

But what these critics – virtually all of whom already own their houses, often having purchased them years ago when prices were lower – don't say is that those cities' slow-growth policies lead to prices that are much higher than they ought to be. Or that such decisions have a cascading effect, as other communities impose their own growth limits until, well, people are grabbing their pitchforks to chase away newcomers to an Idaho city 600 miles from the coast.

The San Diego Builders Association points out that 40% of the price of a new single-family house in San Diego County is attributable to government fees and regulations. That's astonishing. With median prices there nearing $900,000, that means a level of additional cost ($360,000) that would pay for a median-priced home in a major city elsewhere in the country.[10]

Some of those costs are the result of direct fees, but much of the problem is regulatory in nature. By reducing the amount of developable land, regulators increase the price of the remaining buildable tracts. So, sure, no one has a right to live near San Diego's coast – but let's not pretend people are being priced out purely by market forces.[11]

One of the best examples of how dramatically these rules affect building starts took place in 2008 after the financial crash obliterated many nationwide housing markets. The housing crash was caused, of course, by a variety of national financial matters – including the easy lending practices and packaging of high-risk loans into Structured Investment Vehicles that were foisted on unknowing investors. The movie, "The Big Short," provided remarkable insight into a financial implosion that caused housing prices to crash by more than 50% in some inland California markets such as Stockton, Palmdale, Fresno and Desert Hot Springs.[12]

Note, however, that the same bad financial practices affected home markets across the country. Yet the results were not the same everywhere. "California and Florida housing bubbled, but Georgia and Texas housing did not," explained the Cato Institute's Randal O'Toole. "This is hardly because people don't want to live in Georgia and Texas: since 2000, Atlanta, Dallas-Ft. Worth, and Houston have been the nation's fastest-growing urban areas, each growing by more than 120,000 people per year."[13]

Instead, he points to regional factors as "a necessary condition for the housing bubbles where they took place. The most important factor that distinguishes states like California and Florida from states like Georgia and Texas is the amount of regulation imposed on landowners and developers, and in particular a regulatory system known as *growth management*."[14] In areas with intense growth management, prices inflated excessively because supply couldn't keep up with demand (as building restrictions slowed construction). In states with few growth controls, prices hadn't inflated far beyond demand – so they softened rather than crashed after the underlying financial system collapsed.

In other words, growth controls caused the bubble to inflate – and they likewise are the cause of so much Western price inflation now. Even after sustained price growth in fast-growing Dallas and Atlanta, for instance, median home prices there remain, respectively, at an enviable (by California standards) $400,000 and $417,000.[15] Price inflation is the result of limited supply, which in the West is the result of restrictive land-use policies. Because it takes so long to gain government-building approvals in growth-controlled states, the market simply can't respond to demand.

Unaffordable housing stresses a related problem afflicting California (as well as many other West Coast states) – rampant homelessness. In the second half of this book we'll address this separate but related crisis. Simply put, homelessness is not entirely caused by housing unaffordability. It's a multi-pronged problem driven to a large degree by addiction and mental-health issues. But regions with lower-cost housing have much lower levels of homelessness because a lack of low-cost housing leaves those people on the economic margins with nowhere to go. Homelessness is a social problem that's compounded – often dramatically so – by exorbitant housing prices.[16]

But first, we'll look at how we got here and the specific policies that contributed to California's extreme housing imbalance.

How the Government Created a Crisis

As noted above, the current problem has been in the making for 50 years so there's no one simple solution to roll back the regulatory barriers to housing construction. Some of the barriers are the result of state policy and others are from local and regional obstacles. However, the situation stems from a philosophy that's designed to limit or control growth to promote various environmental and urban-design priorities. Such priorities became dominant in the 1970s.

As *Urbanize Los Angeles* explained in a 2018 article: "California in 1960 was a place on the move. Edmund G. 'Pat' Brown Sr. – who served as the state's governor from 1959-1966 – spearheaded three major initiatives aimed at providing a piece of the California dream for all residents of the state. In doing so, Governor Brown became the architect of modern California."[17]

These include the creation of the California State Water Project to make sure there was water available for a growing population, major transportation projects that vastly expanded the state's freeway system and the California Master Plan for Higher Education to expand the state's university system. "These public investments paid off. In 1960, California had 15 million people. Today we have 40 million people and are the world's fifth-largest economy," the article added.[18]

Well, since publication of that article the state's population actually has dropped,[19] which only reinforces the point the writer was making. It was inevitable that when California embraced the opposite policies – disinvestment in basic infrastructure and slow-growth regulations – that the population would begin to go the other way. Surveys consistently show that California's outmigration is driven by middle-class Californians who want to afford their own home and live in less congested, lower cost-of-living cities.

While Pat Brown deserves much credit for his efforts, he governed in an era that valued growth. During his first two terms (1975-1982), his son, Jerry Brown, governed in a "small is beautiful" manner that captured that era's environmental, anti-growth zeitgeist. In between, Gov. Ronald Reagan, who was far less conservative in his policies as governor than as president, actually signed the "landmark" 1970 law that became anathema to future homebuilding efforts: the California Environmental Quality Act, pronounced see-kwa (CEQA).[20]

Politics are complicated, but there's little doubt that a confluence of political and cultural changes drove a dramatic change in Western housing policy beginning in the early 1970s. Here's a look at some of the ensuing policies that have led to our current housing crisis.

The scourge of CEQA

If every modern California lawmaker who complained about the ill effects of CEQA actually voted to reform it, then this controversial law would have long ceased to be a problem. Even many progressive Democrats acknowledge that the measure is cynically used by special interests and no-growthers to delay, contort and halt building projects. Whenever prominent politicians really want a project to move forward, the first thing they do is pass a CEQA exemption. That's what former Senate President Pro Tempore Darrell Steinberg, now the mayor of Sacramento, did as he sought a new Kings basketball arena in the capital city.[21]

As the California Department of Fish and Wildlife explains, CEQA requires developers to "(d)isclose to the public the significant environmental effects of a proposed discretionary project, through the preparation of an initial study, negative declaration, mitigated negative declaration, or environmental impact report." It's designed to "(p)revent or minimize damage to the environment through development of project alternatives, mitigation measures, and mitigation monitoring." And the law enhances "public participation in the environmental review process through scoping meetings, public notice, public review, hearings, and the judicial process."[22]

That process adds costs in preparing the detailed reports, delays the process by subjecting approvals to a wide environmental review, and provides a review process that allows every conceivable opponent (stakeholders!) to have a say. But the real problem stems from its lawsuit provisions. "CEQA is intentionally designed for broad public enforcement, and in general, anyone who has an environmental concern with a project has the standing to bring a lawsuit if the legal violation they are alleging was raised during the administrative process," the pro-CEQA Planning and Conservation League explains.[23]

The result of such "citizen standing" assures that few projects escape the gaze of potential opponents, who often exact concessions simply by threatening to sue. One well-documented abuse involves construction labor unions, which threaten to tie up a proposed project in the courts unless the developer agrees to a union-only project labor agreement. Such PLAs tend to drive up costs by 25%. Neighbors will sue to stop housing projects simply because they don't want a traffic-causing development near them.

Ironically, CEQA often targets projects that advance California's stated environmental aims. A 2015 study found that nearly half of CEQA lawsuits target publicly funded projects, with transit and renewable energy projects high on the target list. The study by the law firm Holland & Knight found that 80% of the lawsuits were filed against the kind of infill projects the state's environmentalists support. It's also used against senior housing and other projects that have widespread local support.[24]

The firm calls for a variety of reforms that would limit the use of lawsuits. A fledgling initiative campaign would eliminate CEQA lawsuits against housing projects unless they were brought by a district attorney, city attorney or state attorney general.[25] As we'll discuss in the next section, the Legislature has passed new laws that exempt CEQA lawsuits from certain by-right development projects, but the state has thus far refused to seriously consider widespread CEQA reforms. And there's little doubt that CEQA is a major obstacle to housing construction.

Creating the California Coastal Commission

California voters approved in 1972 on a 55% to 45% vote Proposition 20, which created the California Coastal Commission to regulate development along the state's 800-plus mile coastline. Few votes better captured the emerging environmentalist sensibilities of that era – and few laws better epitomized the law of unintended consequences. Because the initiative's provisions only lasted until 1976, the California Legislature then passed the Coastal Act to make them permanent.[26]

This is from the ballot summary: "Sets criteria for and requires submission of plan to Legislature for preservation, protection, restoration and enhancement of environment and ecology of coastal zone, as defined. Establishes permit area within coastal zone as the area between the seaward limits of state jurisdiction and 1,000 yards landward from the mean high tide line, subject to specified exceptions. Prohibits any development within permit area without permit by state or regional commission. Prescribes standards for issuance or denial of permits."

Voters no doubt envisioned a commission that would oversee environmental protections at the shoreline, but the commission grabbed the authority to regulate construction decisions as much as five miles inland and into the coastal ranges. Not surprisingly, the commission has long had an almost religious-like no-growth mission. Its original executive director, Peter Douglas who wrote the initiative, has a treasure trove of quotations taking issue with our nation's system of property rights. It's hard to understate the effect of the commission's philosophy – and power – on the state's ability to grow. Recently, the commission voted unanimously to halt a proposed Huntington Beach desalination plant over its concerns about plankton.[27]

"Under Douglas's leadership, the commission became the rogue agency that it is, running roughshod over people's rights, destroying economic opportunity and, ironically, making it unaffordable for all but the wealthiest to buy land in California's coastal zone," Paul Beard (formerly with the Pacific Legal Foundation) told the *New York Times* following Douglas' death in 2012. Bottom line: The commission has consistently opposed new projects, including housing, throughout the coastal zone.[28]

Proposition 13 and its unintended consequences

Even good initiatives have unintended consequences. We're supporters of 1978's Proposition 13, which capped tax rates at 1% of its value at the time of sale and limited increases to 2% a year. At the time, many older Californians in particular were being taxed out of their homes as rapid home appreciation led to rapid appreciation in homeowners' tax bills. The Tax Revolt of 1978 put limits on a ravenous state government and helped pave the way for Ronald Reagan's historic presidency.

Despite opponents' threats of obliterated public services, Proposition 13 didn't actually reduce the government's tax take. For instance, school spending and local government spending per capita is far higher now, adjusted for inflation, than it was before its passage.[29] It did, however, change the way governments collect revenue and the way homeowners behaved. Proposition 13 reduced property turnover by discouraging long-time homeowners from selling given that they would (in most cases) have to give up their capped tax rates and pay at the sales price of the new property.

More significantly, the measure – and follow-up initiatives and laws – discouraged localities from approving housing projects because they came to view the new projects as a financial drain rather than a boon. A 2016 report from the Legislative Analyst's Office outlined that point:

> Proposition 13 altered the fiscal effects of development for local governments in two key ways. First, the property tax allocation system created to implement Proposition 13 provides many cities and counties only a small portion of local property tax revenues. Second … since Proposition 13's passage local governments have become increasingly reliant on other taxes, such as sales and hotel taxes. Because of these changes, many cities and counties find that developments that generate sales or hotel taxes in addition to property taxes yield the highest net fiscal benefits. In contrast, housing developments, which do not produce sales or hotel tax revenues directly, often lead to more local costs than offsetting tax revenues.[30]

Over the years, some lawmakers have proposed various revenue-neutral tax swap plans to mitigate some of those questionable incentives, but re-ordering the state's complex tax code has never gotten much political support for the obvious dangers of potentially touching the state's Third Rail of Politics, as Prop. 13 often is described. But while Proposition 13 has been a blessing in many ways, it also spawned a more aggressive use of the state's redevelopment agencies, which local governments used as a work around to boost city coffers by promoting retail development at the expense of housing.

The subsequent abuse of redevelopment agencies

Formed in the 1940s to combat urban blight, California's redevelopment agencies involved a complex tax-increment financing scheme to promote investment in blighted areas. Local agencies would float debt to pay for infrastructure improvements in a targeted downtrodden project area, and then the tax increment – the growth in property taxes following the completion of the redevelopment project – would pay off the debt. Local agencies would hand pick the developer and often used eminent domain to clear away "blighted" properties.[31]

Post Proposition 13, local government agencies started using their agencies more as a revenue-generating mechanism than a blight-fighting tool. In a quest for tax dollars, agencies began subsidizing shopping malls, movie theaters, auto malls and commercial developments because cities could divert part of the sales-tax take into their discretionary budgets. The result on housing was pronounced: City officials preferred to see vacant tracts turned into tax-generating hotels or shopping centers rather than service-demanding housing developments.

Redevelopment's supporters responded by mentioning the law's requirement that 20% of RDA budgets go toward building "affordable housing." But as Scott Beyer, a market-urbanist writer who occasionally writes for the Free Cities Center, noted in a 2019 *Forbes* article, "this money wound up getting spent inefficiently."[32] It went toward $700,000-a-unit projects of the type that were too costly to make a dent in the housing shortage. Often, cities didn't really want to build lower-income housing, so they preferred overly costly projects that didn't add many units or senior housing. Sometimes they gave their RDA housing dollars to neighboring cities.

In 2011, Gov. Jerry Brown eliminated the agencies in the midst of a budget crisis, given that the state had to backfill 13% of its property tax take to local school districts and other agencies that had lost out on the tax-increment diversions.[33] Nevertheless, for decades these agencies suppressed housing construction by incentivizing cities to promote retail. Some of that thinking is changing now, but RDAs encouraged local planners to prioritize retail over housing.

Excluding housing through inclusionary zoning

Beginning in the 1970s, California localities began passing inclusionary zoning rules. As the housing activist group Home for All San Mateo County defines it, "Inclusionary zoning (IZ), also known as inclusionary housing, is a policy that requires a share of new housing development to be affordable to low- or moderate- income households. The cost of developing affordable units is typically offset with a density bonus (an allowance to build more units than would otherwise be permitted). …California is a leader in the application of local inclusionary zoning policies; approximately 170 cities throughout the state have instituted IZ policies."[34]

California's "leadership" with such policies, however, has had deleterious results. An analysis from the Mercatus Center at George Mason University in Virginia found that the inclusionary-zoning policies are beneficial for a tiny group of low-income residents who essentially (often literally as demand for the limited IZ housing outstrips supply) win the lottery – and qualify for a below-market unit. But the group's review of six studies in 2021 found that these policies correspondingly drive up the cost of housing for almost everyone else.[35]

One study found "inclusionary zoning programs drastically reduced overall housing affordability in the California jurisdictions that adopted them. They find that inclusionary zoning reduced housing supply by 7% and increased prices by 20% between 1990 and 2000." Another one concluded these rules pushed housing prices up in their jurisdictions by 2% to 3%.[36] It's not surprising that a government edict requiring builders to provide subsidized units would discourage construction and increase costs, which are spread around to other buyers.

The rise of development-impact fees

We previously mentioned a new initiative campaign, started by Steve Hilton of the bipartisan non-profit Golden Together, that seeks to limit CEQA lawsuits. CEQA is a widely recognized impediment to housing construction, but the second part of the initiative is less widely remarked upon. That involves development fees – the fees government agencies impose on projects to mitigate the project's impact on infrastructure, parks and other public services. The concept is fine, but localities have used the system to shake down developers to fund costly and unrelated projects that go beyond simple impact mitigation.

The proposed initiative makes the salient point: "California agencies have also imposed unprecedented levels of fees and other regulatory compliance costs on new housing: California housing fees are also nearly three times the national average. New homes and apartments can be charged hundreds of thousands of dollars in fees, on top of the cost of land, labor, and building materials."[37] To rein in the fees, the initiative would cap them at 2% of construction costs.

As the League of California Cities has explained in 2003 research on the topic, the impact-fee process goes back to the 1920s, but in the 1970s the California attorney general and courts reduced cities' limitations on such extractions. A 1976 attorney general opinion affirmed "a city's authority to impose an extraction provided it furthers implementation of the city's general plan and bears at least an indirect relationship to impacts created by the proposed development."[38] A 1987 U.S. Supreme Court gave the

California Coastal Commission latitude to demand easements in exchange for a building permit. The cities group also noted that Proposition 13 encouraged cities to rely more heavily on impact fees. The higher the fees, the higher the building costs.

The rise of rent control

As Swedish economist Assar Lindbeck famously wrote, "In many cases rent control appears to be the most efficient technique presently known to destroy a city – except for bombing."[39] That's because in capping the rents property owners can charge, it discourages them from investing in new rental properties, encourages them to convert apartments to condos and discourages them from upgrading the properties. It discourages mobility as tenants tend to stay put in their under-market units.

Because of San Francisco's strict rent controls and nettlesome tenant board, many of the city's landlords simply keep their units vacant. They fear that once they lease them out, they'll never be able to regain control of them. The city has more than 60,000 of these empty houses and apartments – an astounding statistic in a city where rents average $3,300 a month.[40]

While rent control provides reduced rents for those who already have a unit, it drives up the prices of rental housing over time and throughout the rent-controlled region, as we can see years later in the cities that first embraced it. Berkeley became California's first rent-controlled city in 1973. San Francisco passed its ordinance in 1978. Santa Monica followed suit in 1979. Sixteen California cities have a rent-control ordinance, with Santa Ana being the latest to pass one and create a tenant board. California and Oregon passed the nation's first statewide rent-control laws in 2019. A 2018 study by the National Bureau of Economic Research found that San Francisco's rent-control ordinance reduced housing supply by 15% and led to a 5.1% citywide rent increase.[41]

Rent-control backers have repeatedly lost their efforts to impose stricter rent controls at the ballot in California, but they have qualified another measure for the 2024 ballot. This is a persistent problem – and one that will continue to restrain rental markets.

An increase in local growth-control measures

In the 1970s and 1980s, California voters began passing a large number of local growth-control measures that have added to the difficulties of building new housing. Some of these proposals, even in conservative San Joaquin Valley cities such as Lodi, essentially ground new construction to a halt. It's a key reason that California has been building too few housing units a year to keep up with demand.

One 1989 report[42] found that 66 California cities had passed slow-growth measures since 1971. It quoted a *Time* magazine article from 1988 describing the "rage" felt by California residents at rapid development and growth, noting that voters approved 15 of 17 local slow-growth measures that were on the ballot that year. Many of these initiatives function as urban-growth boundaries that place limits on new construction in areas outside a designated green line.

In Lodi, the city in 1991 approved its Growth Management Allocation Ordinance that requires a maximum amount of new housing units to support no more than 2% annual growth in population.[43] The ordinance was approved by the City Council to protect area farmland and "preserve the city's compact urban form." Not surprisingly, home prices in Lodi subsequently soared above the prices in nearby San Joaquin County cities. The city boasts, however, that it maintained a green belt between it and the Stockton metropolis to the south.

Similar results in all urban growth boundaries

The urban-growth boundary concept was first implemented on a large scale in Oregon in 1973, through the passage of Senate Bill 100.[44] The measure – supported by a coalition of urban interests, environmentalists and an agricultural industry upset about sub-urban encroachments – required every urban area in the state to create a green line and restrict "sprawl" development beyond it. In 1979, Portland created the Metro regional government to oversee land-use planning in the three-county metropolitan area.

Urban planners have pointed to Portland as a national model and many take regular pilgrimages there to tout its approach to growth control, transit development and open-space protection. It's been less of a draw in recent years as the city's homelessness crisis has sprawled out of control and as a crime wave has eroded the quality of life. Although the city has repeatedly expanded the boundary, prices for raw land have jumped dramatically within the boundary. The growth boundary also promoted leap-frog developments outside of Metro's planning control.

Studies clearly suggest that it has significantly raised home prices (not to mention eroding property rights). Banning new housing tracts on open land increases the value of existing developable land by design – and infill construction remains much pricier than new construction in outlying areas. It's the same story wherever these boundaries have been created. Portland used to be one of the West Coast's most affordable cities, which no longer is the case.[45] That's the typical result of UGBs.

"During the 10 years between 1990 and 2000, cities with UGBs grew at a slower rate than other California communities, in terms of both their total population and land area," according to report from the University of Michigan's Center for Local, State and Urban Policy. "Additionally, over this same period, housing prices in UGB-adopting communities grew at a much faster rate – as much as 14% higher – than they did in communities without growth boundaries."[46] Yes, when cities restrict development, they get less supply and higher prices.

The rise of New Urbanism and Smart Growth

Urban growth boundaries and other growth controls are part of a planning philosophy that took hold throughout the West in the 1980s. Myriad new environmental and land-use laws and regulations have distorted housing markets, but they didn't come from nowhere. They were the evolution of a new academic trend. To combat urban sprawl – much of which is admittedly unattractive – a new breed of planners began advocating a design philosophy that promoted denser developments, walkable neighborhoods and less car dependence. Supporters billed it as a move back to older city development traditions.

There's nothing wrong with New Urbanism as a design philosophy. In fact, many of its ideas are quite appealing. The Congress for the New Urbanism's charter, for instance, calls for "the restoration of existing urban centers and towns within coherent metropolitan regions, the reconfiguration of sprawling suburbs into communities of real neighborhoods and diverse districts, the conservation of natural environments, and the preservation of our built legacy."[47]

Who doesn't like cohesive neighborhoods, walkable towns and vibrant city centers? The problem is that it also calls for "the restructuring of public policy and development practices" to restrict the use of cars and promote higher densities and open-space preservation. It's one thing for developers to build new communities using this template – and quite another for governments to ban the types of developments that don't conform to these designs.

Ideas have consequences, and these ideas – married to Smart Growth policies that are imposed at the state and local level – filtered their way down to every planning agency. It meant vast restrictions on the approval of new green-field developments and the prioritization of multi-family projects over single homes with yards – even though most Americans prefer the latter. Innumerable local proposals have been re-jiggered by planners to conform to those dictates. For instance, we think of one typical Southern California proposal for a multitude of single-family houses that, at the insistence of New Urbanist-minded planners, was forced into a dense multi-family project with the vast majority of the land set aside as open space rather than as people's yards.

This slow-growth urbanist philosophy also informs governmental decisions at the highest level. A 2001 *New York Times* article covered then-Gov. Gray Davis' ribbon-cutting at a newly built section of the Foothill Freeway 50 miles east of Los Angeles in suburban San Bernardino County. Davis "dedicated the latest section of freeway and declared that the project would be the last."[48] The state was shifting toward mass transit and development focused on transit lines. The state announced that the era of freeway building was over. In the ensuing 22 years, however, California transit use is at historic lows, but the state continues to prioritize its funding rather than road construction to support new housing developments.

One need only consider the Newhall Ranch project proposed north of Los Angeles in Valencia in the mid-1990s. It would provide 21,500 new homes plus assorted commercial and retail development, and was touted as the largest planned master community in North America. It finally received its approvals 20-plus years later. Meanwhile, farther up the 5 Freeway, the courts recently dealt a blow to the Tejon Ranch proposal – another major housing project that has been tied up in the approval process for decades.[49] How many other needed housing projects faced such delays or never moved forward because of planners' hostility to suburban sprawl?

Climate change policy as a barrier to housing

California's recent planning-related priorities center on battling climate change. That feeds into the other philosophies detailed above – namely protecting open space and reducing the size of the urban footprint, which climate-change warriors argue is key to reducing temperatures. It also reinforces that de-emphasis on freeway building and car dependence in favor of the construction of bus lines and railways (as well as the bullet-train boondoggle). These priorities provide obstacles to housing construction – at least to suburban-style development.

Former Gov. Jerry Brown viewed climate change as his signature issue. One example, from when he was the state's attorney general, spotlights how that policy derailed housing construction. In 2007, Brown sued San Bernardino County over its "housing element." As the *Los Angeles Times* reported that year: "The growth blueprint for San Bernardino County, which projects a 25% increase in population by 2030, fails to adequately assess the effects of increased greenhouse gas emissions and other pollutants, California's attorney general alleges in a lawsuit seeking to have the plan thrown out."[50]

The state argued that the county was permitting too many single-family homes. The eventual settlement called for the construction of more high-density developments, fewer single-family neighborhoods, further investments in public transit and a variety of pollution-mitigation measures. At one point, Brown pointed to Marin County as a model of sustainable, climate-change-resistant growth – a severely growth-controlled county with some of the highest median housing prices in the nation as a result.[51]

These are just the latest policies that impede housing construction, even though lawmakers have also loosened up building restrictions for infill projects.

Has the Legislature Finally Gotten the Message?

As the housing crisis spiraled out of control, California's Legislature has passed several far-reaching measures designed to promote housing construction. The leading proponent is Sen. Scott Wiener, a progressive San Francisco Democrat who has nevertheless corralled most of his caucus on behalf of laws that scale back – albeit in a limited manner and with lots of strings attached – some of the regulatory hurdles imposed by local and state officials. Wiener and his YIMBY (Yes In My Back Yard) allies have scored a succession of impressive victories.

Their first major success was Senate Bill 35.[52] Passed in 2017, the law allows streamlined ministerial approvals for housing projects that include affordable-housing quotas and are built on in-fill sites. That typified the initial approach – creating by-right approvals but only for projects favored by state officials. In 2023, the Legislature passed Senate Bill 423,[53] which extends SB 35's provisions for another decade – but also applies the streamlining to market-rate projects and to projects within the Coastal Zone, thus limiting the California Coastal Commission's authority. The legislation also provides additional oversight for San Francisco given that it has the slowest approval process in the state.

The biggest game-changers were Senate Bills 9 and 10.[54] Signed by Gov. Newsom in 2021, SB 9 essentially ends single-family-only zoning throughout California by allowing property owners to build up to two duplexes on their existing lots. Oregon and Washington previously passed similar laws. SB 10 allowed streamlined approvals for mid-rise multi-family housing along transit lines. It's only been a short time since the law went into effect, with recent research showing that the new laws have only resulted in a small number of related permits. The laws are praise-worthy in that they limit CEQA lawsuits and promote deregulation, but much more needs to be done.

"Los Angeles and other California metropolises need abundant housing to become affordable, and they can get it only by empowering private developers to build significant projects," wrote Edward Glaeser and Atta Tarki in a *Los Angeles Times* column in February. "The fundamental flaw of SB 9 is that it allows individual homeowners to add one or two units at most to their properties, and that is no way to build enough housing to increase affordability."[55]

The state also passed a new law that allows developers to build housing on commercially zoned properties – such as at the site of vacant shopping malls and underused parking lots. Another new law limits the ability of local governments to impose parking requirements. Too often, new housing construction is stymied because of the costs associated with building parking garages.

We agree that builders are perfectly capable of reading their own markets and determining the proper number of parking spaces that they should provide.

Furthermore, the state has become particularly aggressive in forcing local governments to permit additional housing under their state-approved housing plans. A weird convergence of liberal coastal cities and some conservative ones such as Huntington Beach in Orange County have fought and even openly defied these requirements.[56] Huntington Beach filed a lawsuit challenging the state's housing element and thus far refused to permit by-right developments under SB 9. The city's legal brief is the poster child for modern-day NIMBYism (Not In My Back Yard), even though it moved forward under the leadership of a Republican mayor and council.

Of course, California progressives haven't suddenly rediscovered the value of the marketplace. Critics are indeed right to note that the goals of these deregulatory measures are transparent – they are designed to achieve New Urbanist and climate-change-battling goals of densifying neighborhood design. State lawmakers haven't loosened up planning requirements for those who want to build outside the urban footprint. We've yet to see how they will react to a new proposal, from Bay Area venture capitalists, to build an entirely new city (to New Urbanist standards, by the way) in a ranching area in Solano County east of the Bay Area and west of the Sacramento region.[57]

Urban infill construction is far more expensive than suburban construction on green fields, so the state won't meet its housing needs by forcing all new housing construction into that form. Still, half a loaf is better than nothing – and the new "by right" development laws provide a template to expand upon.

But while the state Legislature has made modest progress in dealing with encrusted housing regulations, it hasn't made noticeable headway regarding the homelessness situation. It's a complex problem that, as we noted earlier, isn't entirely a housing problem – but high housing prices and tough competition for rental units has created a crisis for people on the economic edge.

What's Driving Homelessness: Housing or Social Problems?

Much ink has been spilled trying to divine the root causes of California's homelessness crisis.

The Stanford Institute for Economic Policy Research (SIEPR) cites "high housing costs, inadequate shelter spaces, deinstitutionalization, and changes in the criminal justice system" as key drivers.[58] According to a September 2019 Council of Economic Advisers (CEA) report on homelessness, "research has shown that individuals with severe mental illness, substance abuse problems, a history of incarceration, low incomes, and weak social ties are most likely to become homeless. Thus, when the prevalence of these factors grow in a community, the rate of homelessness may grow as well."[59]

The last phrase from the CEA report is relevant for California. California's policies are failing with respect to all the risk factors. The policy environment creates economic obstacles that push people into homelessness and make it much more difficult for homeless people to find stable housing. Policies also misalign incentives, which inadvertently promote more unsheltered homeless. The same policies incentivizing homelessness also limit the state's ability to sustainably address the crisis.

Therefore, it is not a question of whether California's homelessness crisis is driven by the state's affordability issues, mental health problems, or drug and alcohol addictions. California has the worst crisis in the country because all these factors are driving the problem. Productively addressing the problem requires an understanding of the obstacles and disincentives facing those who are homeless.

One commonality harming all homeless people is California's housing unaffordability. The state's growing unaffordability is a policy choice, albeit an unintentional one. The latest regional price parities (RPP) data, which measure the differences in prices (i.e., costs) across states and regions,[60] demonstrates that Californians face the second most-expensive cost of living behind Hawaii residents and the most expensive housing costs.[61] The cost unaffordability is even worse in California's large population centers.

While all costs are above average, California's largest driver is excessive rent and housing expenses. As the California Budget & Policy Center put it:

> (F)or housing costs to be considered affordable, a household's total housing costs should not exceed 30% of household income, according to the U.S. Department of Housing and Urban

Development. Households paying more than 30% of income toward housing are considered housing "cost-burdened," and those with housing costs that exceed half of their income are considered "severely cost-burdened." By these standards, more than four in 10 households statewide had unaffordable housing costs in 2017. Furthermore, one in five households across California faced severe housing cost burdens, spending more than half of their income toward housing expenses.[62]

As noted previously, housing is so unaffordable because overly restrictive zoning regulations, abuse of the California Environmental Quality Act (CEQA), burdensome review processes, and ill-advised rent-control policies severely constrain the state's housing supply relative to housing demand. Throw in costly environmental regulations – including the new solar mandate on all new homes – and affordable housing has become an oxymoron for too many Californians. Housing unaffordability was improving following the mortgage crisis, but started becoming unaffordable around 2014. That's the exact same time that California's homeless problem began to worsen. It is likely this correlation is related.

Housing costs are not the only driver of California's unaffordability problem. According to the Council for Community and Economic Research,[63] three California regions qualified for the top 10 most expensive urban areas as of 2020. San Francisco is the third-most expensive (behind only the Manhattan borough of New York City and Honolulu). Oakland is the seventh-most expensive area. Orange County is the eighth-most expensive. These figures are not adjusted for California's high tax burden, which puts Californians at a further disadvantage relative to most other U.S. cities.

The consequence of this elevated cost of living is that California's median income is not as high as it appears. According to the U.S. Census, the median household income in California was $81,575 in 2021, the latest data available as of this writing.[64] This was high enough to be the 11th highest average household income in the country. But these median household income data do not account for the differences in the cost of living between the states.

Adjusting each state's median household income in 2021 for the buying power of that income as measured by the RPPs, California's median household income in 2021 was 11% lower – $72,967. This adjustment also drops California's ranking from the 11th highest income to the 29th highest income in the country. Once adjusted for California's high cost of living, the average Californian household no longer earns an above-average income – they earn a below-average one.

With respect to the homeless crisis, the state's unaffordability pushes significantly more people and families to the edge. Californians, particularly low-income individuals, are more likely to fall into a vicious cycle from unexpected financial burdens or adverse life events that people in other states would be able to successfully navigate. This increased vulnerability to financial shocks manifests itself in a larger number of people who are homeless for economic reasons.

Whether most homelessness is caused by economic reasons, or a much smaller share, too many people are homeless due to economic reasons. With respect to those who remain homeless for economic reasons, their needs will differ substantially from those who remain homeless due to the problems of addiction and mental illness.

The concept of remaining homeless for economic reasons is crucial. The hardships associated with being homeless cause many people who may not have become homeless due to addiction or mental health problems to develop these problems after living on the streets. In such circumstances, addiction is now a driver – typically the primary driver – of their continued homelessness and inability to obtain sustainable housing. The factors that originally drove them to homelessness are no longer the major obstacle. Therefore, the needs of these individuals will be the same as the needs of the people who became homeless due to addictions and/or mental illness. The evidence clearly demonstrates that addiction and mental illness are rife throughout the homeless population.

A study by California Policy Lab at UCLA found 84% of un-sheltered homeless reported a physical health condition, 78% reported a mental health condition, and 75% reported a substance abuse condition.[65] A *Los Angeles Times* review of over 4,000 questionnaires taken by homeless individuals found similar results –

67% of the unsheltered homeless were dealing with substance abuse or mental health problems.[66] Resolving the unsheltered homelessness crisis is, consequently, synonymous with sustainably addressing the problems of mental illness and addiction.

While presumably unintentional, California's policy environment makes these problems more intractable. Take Proposition 47. A seemingly unrelated policy, Prop. 47 reclassified most drug offenses and theft under $950 as misdemeanors rather than felonies.[67] Regardless of intentions, Prop. 47 helps incentivize the rampant problems of shoplifting and stealing that are driving retailers out of business. From a homeless perspective, the law enables people to maintain destructive drug addictions and eliminates opportunities to help those homeless who are suffering from addictions.

While not a California policy per se, a 2018 decision by the federal Ninth Circuit Court of Appeal (*Martin v. Boise*) ruled that Western cities may not enforce anti-camping laws if there are insufficient shelter beds for the homeless. In practice, the case is creating a right to sleep on the street. The homeless can now camp in front of stores and line streets with tents and these takings of private and public spaces cannot be prevented or reversed unless the city has a bed to house them. The result creates an effective subsidy for being homeless. Homeless individuals suffering with mental health issues or substance abuse problems are now able to subsist over the long-term. While subsisting is possible, living on the streets imposes unacceptably high costs on both the homeless and the broader community.

Policymakers are clearly aware of the crisis and have devoted tens of billions of dollars toward addressing it. These expenditures have largely been in vain, unfortunately, as California's policies continue to be guided by the failed "Housing First" approach. Before discussing policies that address the root causes of the homelessness crisis discussed above, the next section discusses why California's current approach continues to fail.

'Housing First' is a Costly Failure

Following the Obama Administration's lead, California has adopted Housing First as its guiding philosophy for addressing the homeless crisis, which was legally declared a crisis in 2016 by Gov. Jerry Brown. Housing First programs are predicated on the belief that a permanent and stable home is the best platform to help people overcome the challenges that led to their homelessness, including the problems of mental illness and addiction.

Therefore, Housing First offers housing (as distinct from shelter) to all homeless without any preconditions (such as sobriety) or other service requirements. Instead, rapidly placing people in *permanent* housing is the primary goal. It originated as a sensible goal for helping mothers with children who were temporarily homeless but became a governmental philosophy that was applied far too broadly.

The state and localities continue to spend successively more money on programs inspired by Housing First. According to the California Interagency Council on Homelessness, in total state-only expenditures on the "35 state programs serving people experiencing homelessness between Fiscal Year 2018-19 and 2020-21" were $9.6 billion, which included "programs aimed at expanding the supply of affordable housing and providing housing and services to people experiencing homelessness."[68] CNN similarly notes that, "California has spent a stunning $17.5 billion trying to combat homelessness" between 2018 and 2022.[69]

Despite these unprecedented expenditures, Housing First has failed California as evidenced by the continued growth in the numbers of unsheltered homeless. It was not always this way. See Figure 1. The total numbers of homeless individuals generally declined in California between 2007 and 2014. As documented in *No Way Home*, the number of homeless in California was declining by 2.8% annually between 2007 and 2014, which was faster than the overall national decline of 1.3%.[70]

Since 2014, California's homeless population has been growing, particularly since 2016 – the official start of Housing First as the guiding philosophy – and now the state faces the largest homeless problem in the country. Unless advocates want to argue that the crisis would have been even worse if not for these programs, Housing First has been feckless at best.

Overall Homeless
California Point-in-Time Count, 2007 – 2023*

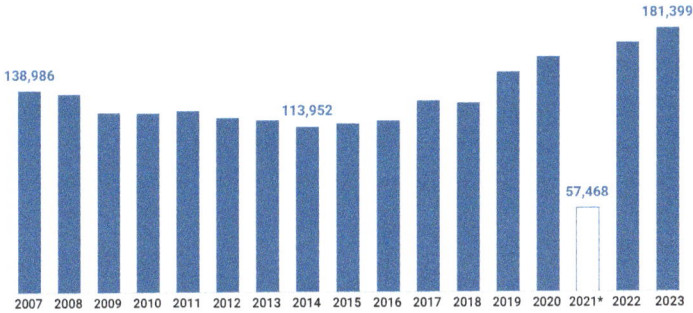

Source: U.S. Department of Housing and Urban Development
* 2021 data were unable to count unsheltered homeless due to the impact from COVID-19.

Take Proposition HHH in Los Angeles as an example, a measure approved by more than 77% of the voters in 2016. Prop HHH authorized $1.2 billion in bonds ($1.9 billion including total debt costs) to fund housing for homeless people and people at risk of becoming homeless as well as facilities that provide mental health care, addiction treatment and other services.

In December 2021, the Los Angeles Controller's office reviewed the measure's performance. The report concluded that problems overshadow progress, particularly the outrageous cost of building affordable housing, which continue to grow every year.[71] In 2020, the average costs to build *affordable* housing in Los Angeles was $531,000, which grew to nearly $600,000 in 2021, with 14% of the units under construction exceeding $700,000 per unit.[72] The review also noted that, compared to the goal of building 10,000 units in 10 years, 1,142 units had been completed in five years.[73] Consistent with statewide trends, the city's homeless population has increased by 45% since HHH was passed.[74]

Project Roomkey/Homekey, California's latest Housing First efforts, provides additional evidence that Housing First is a flawed approach. Project Roomkey was launched in March 2020 in response to the COVID-19 pandemic "to provide non-congregate shelter options for people experiencing homelessness, protect human life, and minimize strain on health care system capacity."[75] By April 2020, Project Roomkey had across the state "secured 10,974 hotel and motel rooms and 1,133 trailers for extremely vulnerable individuals experiencing homelessness, to help flatten the curve and preserve hospital capacity."[76]

Project Homekey, which grew out of Project Roomkey, was created by Assembly Bill 83. Passed in 2020, the law directed state and federal emergency funds to be used to buy hotels and motels, renovate them, and "convert them into permanent, long-term housing for people experiencing homelessness."[77]

Despite its massive expenditures, Project Homekey has severely underperformed based on its own metrics. In Los Angeles, for instance, the goal was to provide 15,000 rooms to shelter the homeless,[78] but, as of August 2020 (the program's high-water mark), only 4,177 rooms had been secured countywide.[79] By the end of June 2021, only 1,794 rooms were occupied.[80] At its conclusion, just 9,118 had gone through the program, and only 2,474 of those were placed into permanent housing; 3,388 made it into interim housing.[81] The costs of Project Roomkey per participant per night came to around $260, many times higher than congregate shelter.[82] On top of it all, throughout the program's implementation, Los Angeles' homeless crisis continued to worsen.

Project Homekey's track record in San Francisco is similarly disappointing. San Francisco received tens of millions of dollars from Project Homekey, including $29.1 million in capital and operating costs to buy a 130-room hotel, $45 million to buy a 232-room hotel,[83] and $54.7 million in state funds that will help the city purchase a 160-room building in the SoMa district to house the homeless.[84] In fiscal year 2021–22 alone, San Francisco spent $1.1 billion on homeless programs.

The city, however, has not shown that it is capable of effectively deploying the resources. Many of the rooms are filthy and infested with rodents. Making matters worse, the communities are plagued with violence, drug use, crime and even deaths from drug overdoses.[85] As the *San Francisco Chronicle* documented, "residents have threatened to kill staff members, chased them with metal pipes" and started fires inside of rooms.[86] The *Chronicle* also documented that at least 166 residents fatally overdosed in city-funded hotels in 2020 and 2021.[87] The broader community continues to suffer from the overall deterioration in the quality of life and economic opportunities.[88]

San Francisco's experience exemplifies the practical problems that often arises when implementing Housing First programs. As a *San Francisco Chronicle* investigation demonstrated, the city simply has a dismal record caring for the residents in the 16 Project Homekey hotels.

First, the Housing First programs are not transitioning people to stable and independent living – the premise of Housing First. Of the 515 Project Homekey residents tracked after leaving permanent supportive housing, 21% returned to homelessness, 27% left for an "unknown destination," and a quarter died while still in the program, leaving only about a quarter living in stable homes, "mostly by moving in with friends or family or into another taxpayer-subsidized building."[89]

Lastly, despite the billions of dollars spent, homelessness in San Francisco continually worsens. Benchmarked against 2016, the year the Department of Homelessness and Supportive Housing was created, the number of homeless people in the city has grown by 56%.[90] Growing numbers of homeless is the expected, yet unfortunate, outcome because Housing First programs fail to address the foundational problems of addiction and mental illness that afflicts most homeless people.[91] As Pacific Research Institute writers document in the book *No Way Home*:

> (R)esidents of Housing First programs show no improvement regarding addiction and mental illness. ... A recent Housing First experiment in Ottawa, Canada, illustrates this paradoxical outcome in stark terms. Researchers divided up the study into two populations: an "intervention" group that was provided Housing First and access to primary care, medically assisted treatment, social workers, and on-demand services; and a non-intervention "control" group that was not provided housing or services – they were simply left on the streets as they

were before. To the shock of the researchers, after 24 months, the non-intervention control group reported better results regarding substance abuse, mental health, quality of life, family relations and mortality than the Housing First group. *In other words, doing nothing resulted in superior human outcomes than providing Housing First with wrap-around services.*[92]

Bringing together all these flaws demonstrates that Housing First policies, while well intentioned, are incapable of resolving California's ever-worsening homelessness. It is simply an ineffective response for those homeless suffering with mental-health issues and addiction and excessively costly for those homeless where it can help.

Housing and Homeless Solutions

If Housing First is not the right approach, then what should California do? Rather than throwing billions more toward the failed Housing First programs, California should implement a comprehensive strategy that efficiently targets the factors perpetuating homelessness.

As much as possible, the state should partner with effective private nonprofit organizations – a practice recognized by both parties to enhance innovativeness. As the Obama Administration's plan to end homelessness acknowledged, "the private and philanthropic sectors are responsible for some of the best thinking, innovation, and evidence-based approaches to ending homelessness."[93]

Private organizations have a successful track record of efficiently addressing the root causes driving an individual's homelessness and then transitioning homeless individuals off the streets. Of particular interest should also be organizations that offer a compelling and measurable, value-added service such as the ability to develop low-cost transitional shelters.

One private organization providing innovative solutions to transition homeless individuals into sustainable housing is Entryway. The Vienna, Va., nonprofit "transitions individuals and families at risk of or experiencing homelessness to economic self-sufficiency by providing career training, full-time employment and housing opportunities in partnership with the real estate industry."[94] Their holistic approach would be particularly valuable for those Californians who remain homeless for economic reasons.

There is a catch in California. As reviewed in the section "What's Driving Homelessness," too many of the state's current policies unnecessarily drive up the cost of living in the state. Among the 100 largest cities in the United States, rent in California's cities are approximately 50% higher for one-bedroom and two-bedroom apartments, according to Zumper's 2023 National Rent Report.[95] These excess costs harm everyone but impose a much higher burden on lower-income families and create additional obstacles for individuals who are trying to transition from homelessness to economic self-sufficiency. An income that would enable someone to comfortably live in Virginia (where Entryway is headquartered) would still leave that person economically insecure throughout most of California.

Table 1
Average Rent Top 50 Cities by Population
California versus Cities Outside of California

City	Average 1-Bedroom Rent	Average 2-Bedroom Rent
California Cities	$2,047	$2,664
Top 100 Cities Outside California	$1,414	$1,749
California Premium	44.8%	52.3%

Source: Zumper National Rent Report

Consequently, California's policy-created affordability crisis is both a cause of the homelessness crisis and an obstacle to resolving it. Comprehensive regulatory reforms can relieve families of the unnecessary costs driving California's affordability problems. Beneficial reforms would revise the overly restrictive local zoning laws to incentivize the construction of more homes – particularly multi-family homes. As discussed above, the state can play an even more important role by reforming (or ideally eliminating) CEQA.[96] The supply shortages caused by these regulations unnecessarily drive-up housing costs to unaffordable levels.

But it is not just housing that is unaffordable in California. Other regulations, particularly the state's energy and global climate change policies, drive up energy costs, which are the highest in the continental United States. Due to energy's ubiquitous use, higher energy costs drive up the costs of most other goods and services in the state, including core necessities. All these higher costs make it harder for lower-income and working-class families to thrive in the state. With respect to the homeless crisis, California's higher overall cost of living exacerbates the problems created by its unaffordable housing crisis.

There is good news: because ill-advised policies cause the problems, policy reforms can alleviate them. These reforms should focus on eliminating the policy-created energy costs by repealing the mandates for solar panels and electric vehicles that force consumers to purchase more expensive products regardless of their financial position. The costs of energy can also be moderated by removing the favoritism toward electricity generation sources that are politically favored, but economically and generationally deficient.

California's embrace of the Housing First philosophy also creates unnecessary barriers. The focus on building *permanent* housing is problematic because the state cannot possibly build enough housing for the homeless at such high per-unit costs. But private organizations, such as DignityMoves, have succeeded in building temporary supportive housing.[97] There are several advantages this type of private organization offers compared to the current government-driven solutions.

First, as demonstrated with the communities that have already been built, DignityMoves demonstrates that private organizations can be nimbler and are incentivized to be more innovative.

Second, the organization can tailor the solutions to the needs of specific communities. Third, the focus on temporary housing creates benefits that the government's focus on permanent housing cannot match. Rather than spending between $700,000 and $800,000 to build one permanent housing unit, DignityMoves can build each unit (including supportive facilities) for $50,000. The units can be moved, so DignityMoves communities are flexible and can be moved to reflect the evolving needs of supportive housing.

Reducing the costs for building supportive housing creates another important benefit – it frees up resources, which can be dedicated toward the necessary support services. Sustainably resolving the homelessness crisis requires programs that address the social problems afflicting most homeless people. Of particular importance is addressing the critical issues of addiction and mental health.

Given the state's poor track record running these programs, ideally the state would leverage the successful private nonprofit organizations that efficiently address the root causes of homelessness. One example is Father Joe's Villages in San Diego,[98] which provides homeless people with comprehensive services including emergency shelter, medical care, mental health treatment, job skills training and ongoing support. Emphasizing the efficiency of their operations, Father Joe's Villages notes that, "watchdog organizations say that top-rated charities should spend at least 75% of their budget on services. Father Joe's Villages works hard to ensure that as much as your money as possible goes directly to programs helping our neighbors in need. That's why 86% of our combined revenue goes directly towards our life-changing programs and services."[99]

The state should focus on efficiently delivering services to help homeless individuals address addiction and mental-health issues. Toward this end, the state should evaluate the benefits from greater reliance on state mental hospitals that are dedicated to serving this population.[100] The alternative of providing mental-health treatment from a Housing First platform is proving to be ineffective and costly.

In addition to improving the services infrastructure, the state should both create opportunities to transition homeless to the effective services and turn negative interactions with the state into opportunities to help. One strategy, employed by Crossroads Welcome Center in Tennessee, will initiate contact with the homeless by using day rooms to provide necessities, including bag storage, transportation, Internet access and a sitting room.[101] While offering these services, day center staff can determine each client's needs and try to direct them to institutions for further care.

Day rooms create positive interactions where staff can help transition homeless individuals to the appropriate services, but not all interactions will be positive. Many interactions will arise when homeless individuals commit crimes. Broadly implementing homeless courts that can "sentence" people who are experiencing homelessness and either suffering from addiction or mental illness to treatment rather than incarceration enable California to turn criminal infractions into opportunities to help.

In a positive sign, the use and support of homeless courts continues to grow. As the California courts noted, "there are currently homeless court programs in 19 California counties. Most of the existing courts are held at least monthly with many holding court weekly."[102] Expanding these courts to all counties and holding court more often can accelerate the benefits. A new statewide CARE Courts program is soon coming online.

Of course, homeless courts can only work when the state and local governments enforce laws against theft. While likely requiring initiatives that would include repealing or significantly reforming Proposition 47, homeless courts offer the ability to both improve the quality of life in California's cities and help the homeless transition to the help and support they need.

With these strategies in place, the state would be better positioned to actively discourage homeless encampments. In fact, a proliferation of low-cost temporary housing enabled by organizations like DignityMoves can ensure that enforcing no-camping laws complies with the *Martin v. Boise* ruling – there would be sufficient beds available. The benefits from eliminating the encampments can be further enhanced by promoting a high quality-of-life standard for all neighborhoods that includes eliminating the open-air drug markets and disregard for laws big and small.

From a broad perspective, California can more effectively address the homelessness crisis by focusing on building more cost-effective temporary housing, prioritizing treatment first before transitioning to permanent housing, leveraging more efficient private-sector groups to provide the essential support services, repealing the regulations that are driving the state's affordability crisis and enforcing the law.

Such an approach will not only help alleviate the current homelessness crisis, but will also improve the quality of life for Californians and enhance the economic viability of cities across the state.

Conclusion: The Strategy Moving Forward

Policymakers throughout California and the West seem to forget that that the law of supply and demand applies to housing markets as well as every other part of the economy. The source of our unaffordability crisis is remarkably simple. This is the conclusion from that previously mentioned 2015 LAO report, which calls for additional building to meet demand:

> California is a desirable place to live. Yet not enough housing exists in the state's major coastal communities to accommodate all of the households that want to live there. In these areas, community resistance to housing, environmental policies, lack of fiscal incentives for local governments to approve housing, and limited land constrains new housing construction. A shortage of housing along California's coast means households wishing to live there compete for limited housing. This competition bids up home prices and rents. Some people who find California's coast unaffordable turn instead to California's in-

> land communities, causing prices there to rise as
> well. In addition to a shortage of housing, high land
> and construction costs also play some role in high
> housing prices.[103]

As noted earlier, the state has embraced some deregulatory policies that will help boost supply – but the new laws are applied only in targeted areas. The state needs to build a broad consensus for rolling back construction barriers in all regions and on undeveloped areas as well as infill sites. It took several decades to get to this crisis point, so there's no one easy button to reverse the complex interaction of regulations, fees, lawsuits and slow-growth ideologies.

Regarding homelessness, the answers aren't quite as simple, even though we tried to detail some promising public- and private-based alternatives. But loosening housing-construction rules will take pressure off of the entire market and open up opportunities at the lower rungs of the housing ladder. Easing off slow-growth restrictions will also make it easier for nonprofits to build temporary and transitional housing that benefits the homeless. The state also needs to stop squandering its resources on programs that don't work, such as Housing First, and earmarking them toward projects that can provide real help for our poorest residents. There's much more to dealing with the homeless crisis than increasing housing supply, but that will really help.

"Homelessness isn't just an issue in San Francisco," said San Francisco Mayor London Breed.[104] "It's an issue throughout California and up and down the West Coast. We need to support policies that address our twin troubles of housing affordability and homelessness at the state-level." While the Mayor's observation may not be particularly groundbreaking, it happens to be true. The two issues remain intertwined. We can start to address those twin troubles by rolling back policies that make it inordinately difficult and expensive to build new housing.

Endnotes

1   Jason Burger, "Home Price Differential," *Los Angeles Times*, Oct. 28, 1990, https://www.latimes.com/archives/la-xpm-1990-10-28-re-4506-story.html

2   Christian Leonard, "Buying a San Francisco home took 3 years of income in 1970. Here's today's number," *San Francisco Chronicle*, Sept. 18, 2023, https://www.sfchronicle.com/realestate/article/home-price-income-18367360.php#:~:text=That%20wasn't%20an%20insignificant,household%20income%20and%20home%20values.

3   San Francisco Housing Market, Redfin, https://www.redfin.com/city/17151/CA/San-Francisco/housing-market, accessed Sept. 24, 2023

4   Mark Strassmann, "The least affordable housing market in the U.S.? Boise," CBS News, Dec. 3, 2021, https://www.cbsnews.com/news/housing-market-boise-idaho-least-affordable/

5   Maria L. La Ganga, "'Go back to California': Wave of newcomers fuels backlash in Boise," *Los Angeles Times*, Nov. 10, 2019, https://www.latimes.com/california/story/2019-11-10/go-back-to-california-wave-of-newcomers-fuels-backlash-in-boise

6   Ibid.

7   Margaret Carmel, "Density 'applied strategically': Boise backtracks on citywide upzone in new zoning code proposal," *BoiseDev*, July 13, 2022, https://boisedev.com/news/2022/07/13/boise-zoning-code-rewrite/

8   Mac Taylor, "California's High Housing Costs," Legislative Analyst's Office, March 17, 2015, https://lao.ca.gov/reports/2015/finance/housing-costs/housing-costs.pdf

9   Ibid.

10   Roger Showley, "Regulation adds 40% to housing prices, study shows," *San Diego Union-Tribune*, April 19, 2015, https://www.sandiegouniontribune.com/business/growth-development/sdut-housing-regulation-cost-nazarene-2015apr29-htmlstory.html

11   Ibid.

12   L. Franklin Devine and Jennifer MacDonald, "House of Cards: The Mortgage Mess," CBS News, Jan. 25, 2008, https://www.cbsnews.com/news/house-of-cards-the-mortgage-mess/

13   Randal O'Toole, "How Urban Planners Caused the Housing Bubble," Cato Institute Policy Analysis, Oct. 1, 2009, https://www.cato.org/policy-analysis/how-urban-planners-caused-housing-bubble

14   Ibid.

15   Redfin, https://www.redfin.com/city/30756/GA/Atlanta/housing-market

16   Free Cities Center video interview with Jim Palmer, former president of the Orange County Rescue Mission, https://www.pacificresearch.org/oc-rescue-mission-how-a-private-charity-is-turning-around-lives-more-effectively-than-government/

17   Hunter Kerhart, "Everyone Deserves the California Dream. It's Time We Build Enough Housing to Provide It," *Urbanize Los Angeles*, Jan. 31, 2018, https://la.urbanize.city/post/everyone-deserves-california-dream-its-time-we-build-enough-housing-provide-it

18   Ibid.

19   Ben Christopher, "California's persistently shrinking population," *CALmatters*, Feb. 17, 2023, https://calmatters.org/newsletters/whatmatters/2023/02/california-population-exodus-housing/#:~:text=In%202021%2C%20it%20was%20big,April%202020%20and%20July%202022.

20   Dan Farber, "Ronald Reagan – Environmentalist Governor," *Legal Planet*, Jan. 20, 2016, https://legal-planet.org/2016/06/20/ronald-reagan-environmentalist-governor/

21   Anthony York, "Sacramento lawmakers seek last-minute CEQA exemption for Kings arena," *Los Angeles Times*, Aug. 30, 2013, https://www.latimes.com/local/political/la-me-pc-sacramento-kings-ceqa-downtown-arena-kevin-johnson-20130829-story.html

22   California Department of Fish and Wildlife, "California Environmental Quality Act Review," https://wildlife.ca.gov/Conservation/Environmental-Review/CEQA, accessed Sept. 24, 2023

23 Planning and Conservation League, "CEQA FAQs," https://www.pcl.org/campaigns/ceqa/ceqa-faqs/, accessed Sept. 24, 2023.

24 Jennifer Hernandez, "In the Name of the Environment Part III: CEQA, Housing, and the Rule of Law," examines CEQA lawsuits filed in state courts over a period of three years, between 2019-21," Chapman University, May 26, 2023, https://www.hklaw.com/en/news/pressreleases/2023/05/ceqa-lawsuits-remain-a-roadblock-to-housing

25 Steve Hilton, "A plan to restore the California dream," *The Orange County Register,* Sept. 6, 2023, https://www.ocregister.com/2023/09/06/steve-hilton-a-plan-to-restore-the-california-dream/

26 "An Introduction to the California Coastal Act, the California Coastal Commission, https://www.coastal.ca.gov/coastalvoices/IntroductionToCoastalAct.pdf, accessed Sept. 24, 2023

27 Rachel Becker, "A salty dispute: California Coastal Commission unanimously rejects desalination plant," *CALmatters*, May 12, 2022, https://calmatters.org/environment/2022/05/california-desalination-plant-coastal-commission/

28 Dennis Hevesi, "Peter Douglas, Sentry of California's Coast, Dies at 69," *New York Times*, https://www.nytimes.com/2012/04/09/us/peter-douglas-defender-of-california-coast-dies-at-69.html#:~:text=Paul%20Beard%2C%20head%20of%20the,land%20in%20California's%20coastal%20zone.%E2%80%9D

29 Jon Coupal, "Sorry naysayers -- Prop. 13 is still working after all these years," Howard Jarvis Taxpayers Association, Spring 2023, https://www.hjta.org/news-events/taxing-times-online-spring-2023/presidents-message/

30 Mac Taylor, "Common Claims about Proposition 13," Legislative Analyst's Office, Sept. 19, 2016, https://lao.ca.gov/publications/report/3497

31 Steven Greenhut, "Proving the Redevelopment Rule," *City Journal*, June 13, 2011, https://www.city-journal.org/article/proving-the-redevelopment-rule

32 Scott Beyer, "California's Redevelopment Agencies: The Bad Idea That Won't Die," *Forbes*, Feb. 13, 2019, https://www.forbes.com/sites/scottbeyer/2019/02/13/californias-redevelopment-agencies-the-bad-idea-that-wont-die/?sh=7c2ef4065396

33 Simone Wilson, "Redevelopment agencies across California, including L.A. CRA, abolished," *LA Weekly,* Dec. 29, 2011, https://www.laweekly.com/redevelopment-agencies-across-california-including-l-a-cra-abolished-governor-jerry-brown-victorious/

34 Home for All San Mateo County, "Inclusionary Zoning (IZ)," https://homeforallsmc.org/toolkits/inclusionary-zoning/#:~:text=Inclusionary%20zoning%20(IZ)%2C%20also,%2D%20or%20moderate%2D%20income%20households, accessed Sept. 24, 2023

35 Emily Hamilton, "Inclusionary zoning hurts more than it helps," Mercatus Center, Feb. 8, 2021, https://www.mercatus.org/research/policy-briefs/inclusionary-zoning-hurts-more-it-helps

36   Ibid.

37   Steve Hilton, "A plan to restore the California dream," *The Orange County Register,* Sept. 6, 2023, https://www.ocregister.com/2023/09/06/steve-hilton-a-plan-to-restore-the-california-dream/

38   Peter Brown and Graham Lyons, "A Short Overview of Development Impact Fees," League of California Cities, 2003 Continuing Education Program, https://www.cacities.org/UploadedFiles/LeagueInternet/d7/d7ce5783-7207-4236-a5fe-3352da30f8f0.pdf

39   David Henderson, "Rent Control is Worse than Bombing," *EconLib*, March 5, 2019, https://www.econlib.org/rent-control-is-worse-than-bombing/

40   Amy Larson, "61,000 homes are vacant in San Francisco: report," KRON, Oct. 20, 2022, https://www.kron4.com/news/bay-area/61000-homes-are-empty-in-san-francisco-report/#:~:text=The%20number%20of%20vacant%20homes,the%20country%2C%20the%20report%20found.

41   Rebecca Diamond, Timothy McQuade and Franklin Qian, "The Effects of Rent Control Expansion on Tenants, Landlords, and Inequality: Evidence from San Francisco," National Bureau of Economic Research, January 2018, https://www.nber.org/papers/w24181

42   Daniel J. Curtin Jr. and M. Thomas Jacobson, "Growth Management by the Initiative in California: Legal and Practical Issues," *The Urban Lawyer*, 1989, https://www.jstor.org/stable/27894622

43   City of Lodi, "Growth Management and Infrastructure,"
      https://www.lodi.gov/DocumentCenter/View/191/Chap-
      ter-3---Growth-Management-and-Infrustructure-PDF,
      accessed Sept. 24, 2023

44   Senate Bill 100, Oregon Encyclopedia, https://www.ore-
      gonencyclopedia.org/articles/senate_bill_100/

45   Scott Beyer, "Portland's Urban Growth Boundary: A
      Driver of Suburban Sprawl," *Forbes*, March 29, 2017,
      https://www.forbes.com/sites/scottbeyer/2017/03/29/
      portlands-urban-growth-boundary-a-driver-of-suburban-
      sprawl/?sh=38d65c356964

46   Elizabeth R. Gerber and Justin H. Phillips, "Growth Man-
      agement Policy in California Communities," University of
      Michigan Center for Local, State, and Urban Policy, April
      2004, https://closup.umich.edu/research/policy-reports/
      growth-management-policy-california-communities

47   Charter of the Congress for the New Urbanism, https://
      www.cnu.org/who-we-are/charter-new-urbanism#:~:-
      text=The%20Congress%20for%20the%20New,one%20
      interrelated%20community%2Dbuilding%20challenge,
      accessed Sept. 24, 2023.

48   James Sterngold, "California Governor Sees an End to
      Freeway Building," *The New York Times*, Aug. 21, 2001,
      https://www.nytimes.com/2001/08/21/us/california-gov-
      ernor-sees-an-end-to-freeway-building.html

49   Trevor Bach, "Judge deals deadly blow to Tejon Ranch
      master plan," *The Real Deal*, March 29, 2023, https://the-
      realdeal.com/la/2023/03/29/judge-deals-deadly-blow-to-
      tejon-ranch-master-plan/

50   Tim Reiterman, "State sues San Bernardino County to nullify its blueprint for growth," *Los Angeles Times*, April 14, 2007, https://www.latimes.com/archives/la-xpm-2007-apr-14-me-berdoo14-story.html

51   Steven Greenhut, "Jerry Brown: older, not wiser," *The Orange County Register*, April 4, 2010, https://www.ocregister.com/2010/04/04/steven-greenhut-jerry-brown-older-not-wiser/

52   Senate Bill 35, California Legislative Information, https://leginfo.legislature.ca.gov/faces/billNavClient.xhtml?bill_id=201720180SB35

53   Senate Bill 423, California Legislative Information, https://leginfo.legislature.ca.gov/faces/billNavClient.xhtml?bill_id=202320240SB423

54   Steven Greenhut, "California's Land-Use Reforms Promote Freedom and Property Rights," *Reason*, Sept. 3, 2021, https://reason.com/2021/09/03/californias-land-use-reforms-promote-freedom-and-property-rights/

55   Edward Glaeser and Atta Tarki, "California housing development remains abysmal despite reforms. Here's what's missing," *Los Angeles Times*, Feb. 18, 2023, https://www.latimes.com/opinion/story/2023-02-19/california-housing-developers-los-angeles#:~:text=In%201970%2C%20the%20median%20owner,with%20an%20increasingly%20fixed%20supply.

56   Editorial, "NIMBY cities like Huntington Beach need to let more housing get built," *The Orange County Register*, May 18, 2023, https://www.ocregister.com/2023/05/18/nimby-cities-need-to-let-homes-get-built/

57   Edward Ring, "How new city can change how California
      envisions its future," Free Cities Center, Sept. 22, 2023,
      https://www.pacificresearch.org/how-new-city-can-
      change-how-california-envisions-its-future-part-one/

58   Jialu L. Streeter, "Homelessness in California: Causes and
      Policy Considerations," SIEPR, May 2022, https://siepr.
      stanford.edu/publications/policy-brief/homelessness-cali-
      fornia-causes-and-policy-considerations.

59   "The State of Homelessness in America" Council of Eco-
      nomic Advisers, September 2019, https://www.nhipdata.
      org/local/upload/file/The-State-of-Homelessness-in-
      America.pdf.

60   "Regional Price Parities by State and Metro Area," Bureau
      of Economic Analysis, https://www.bea.gov/data/pric-
      es-inflation/regional-price-parities-state-and-metro-area.

61   "Regional Price Parities by State and Metro Area," Bu-
      reau of Economic Analysis, https://www.bea.gov/data/
      prices-inflation/regional-price-parities-state-and-met-
      ro-area#:~:text=Regional%20price%20parities%20
      (RPPs)%20measure,the%20overall%20national%20
      price%20level. (accessed July 13, 2023).

62   Sara Kimberlin, "California's Housing Affordability
      Crisis Hits Renters and Households With the Lowest
      Incomes the Hardest," California Budget & Policy Center,
      April 2019, https://calbudgetcenter.org/wp-content/
      uploads/2019/04/Report_California-Housing-Affordabil-
      ity-Crisis-Hits-Renters-and-Households-With-the-Low-
      est-Incomes-the-Hardest_04.2019.pdf.

63 The Council of Community and Economic Research maintains a Cost-of-Living Index that ranks regions based on the "cost of consumer goods and services, excluding taxes and non-consumer expenditures; see: Annual 2020 Cost of Living Index Release, Council of Community and Economic Research, March 2021. The index measures the relative cost for more than "90,000 prices covering almost 60 different items," from "housing, utilities, grocery items, transportation, health care, and miscellaneous goods and services."

64 See: U.S. Census Income Tables: https://www.census.gov/topics/income-poverty/income.html (accessed August 15, 2023).

65 Janey Rountree, Nathan Hess, and Austin Lyke, "Health Conditions Among Unsheltered Adults in the U.S.", California Policy Lab Policy Brief, October 2019, https://www.capolicylab.org/wp-content/uploads/2023/02/Health-Conditions-Among-Unsheltered-Adults-in-the-U.S..pdf.

66 Doug Smith and Benjamin Oreskes, "Are many homeless people in L.A. mentally ill? New findings back the public's perception," *Los Angeles Times*, October 7, 2019, https://www.latimes.com/california/story/2019-10-07/homeless-population-mental-illness-disability.

67 "Prop 47 Resentencing" https://www.nevada.courts.ca.gov/divisions/criminal-misdemeanor/prop-47-resentencing#:~:text=Prop%2047%20Resentencing%20Information&text=This%20Act%20reduces%20most%20drug,-for%20resentencing%20as%20a%20misdemeanor.

68   "Statewide Homelessness Assessment (July 1, 2018 – June 30, 2021), Report to the Legislature Pursuant to Assembly Bill 140 (Chapter 111, Statutes of 2021)" California Interagency Council on Homelessness, https://bcsh.ca.gov/calich/documents/homelessness_assessment.pdf.

69   Nick Watt, "California has spent billions to fight homelessness. The problem has gotten worse," CNN, July 11, 2023, https://www.cnn.com/2023/07/11/us/california-homeless-spending/index.html.

70   Kerry Jackson, Christopher Rufo, Joseph Tartakovsky, and Wayne Winegarden, *No Way Home: The Crisis of Homelessness and How to Fix It with Intelligence and Humanity*, Encounter Books March 16, 2021

71   "The Problems and Progress of Prop. HHH," Ron Galperin, Los Angeles controller, February 23, 2022, available at https://wpstaticarchive.lacontroller.io/wp-content/uploads/2022/02/2.22.23_The-Problems-and-Progress-of-Prop-HHH_Final.pdf

72   Ibid.

73   Ibid.

74   M. Nolan Gray, "Los Angeles' Campaign To End Homelessness Isn't Working. What Now?" Pacific Research Institute, *Right By The Bay*, available at https://www.pacificresearch.org/los-angeles-campaign-to-end-homelessness-isnt-working-what-now/

75   "Project Roomkey/Housing and Homelessness COVID Response," Department of Social Services, available at https://www.cdss.ca.gov/inforesources/cdss-programs/housing-programs/project-roomkey

76 "Governor Newsom Visits Project Roomkey Site in Santa Clara County to Highlight Progress on the State's Initiative to Protect Homeless Individuals from COVID-19," Office of Governor Gavin Newsom, April 18, 2020, available at https://www.gov.ca.gov/2020/04/18/governor-newsom-visits-project-roomkey-site-in-santa-clara-county-to-highlight-progress-on-the-states-initiative-to-protect-homeless-individuals-from-covid-19/

77 Frequently Asked Questions about Homekey," County of Los Angeles, available at https://lacounty.gov/homekey/

78 "Project Roomkey is Failing in Los Angeles–Now We Know Why," *KNOCKLA,* September 15, 2020, available at https://knock-la.com/homeless-los-angeles-project-roomkey-lahsa-12027aafec7b/

79 Ibid.

80 Project Roomkey Tracker, available at https://projectroomkeytracker.com/

81 "Project Roomkey Fell Short Of Expectations In LA County, Experts Say," CBS Los Angeles, September 29, 2021, available at https://www.cbsnews.com/losangeles/news/project-roomkey-fell-short-of-expectations-in-la-county-experts-say/

82 Ibid.

83 "San Francisco Awarded $29 Million from State's Project Homekey for Purchase of 130-room Hotel for Homeless Housing" Office Mayor London N. Breed, October 23, 2020, available at https://sfmayor.org/article/san-francisco-awarded-29-million-states-project-homekey-purchase-130-room-hotel-homeless

84   J.D. Morris, "San Francisco gets $54.7 million to buy SoMa building for homeless housing," *San Francisco Chronicle*, December 24, 2021, available at https://www.sfchronicle.com/bayarea/article/San-Francisco-gets-54-7-million-to-buy-SoMa-16721040.php

85   Joaquin Palomino, Trisha Thadani, "Broken Homes," *San Francisco Chronicle*, April 26, 2022, available at https://www.sfchronicle.com/projects/2022/san-francisco-sros/

86   Ibid.

87   Ibid.

88   Lee Ohanian, "Despite Spending $1.1 Billion, San Francisco Sees Its Homelessness Problems Sprial Out Of Control," *California on Your Mind*, Hoover Institution, May 10, 2022, available at https://www.hoover.org/research/despite-spending-11-billion-san-francisco-sees-its-homelessness-problems-spiral-out-control

89   Joaquin Palomino, Trisha Thadani, "Broken Homes," *San Francisco Chronicle*, April 26, 2022, available at https://www.sfchronicle.com/projects/2022/san-francisco-sros/

90   Ibid.

91   See the survey data cited in the previous chapter "What's Driving Homelessness."

92   Kerry Jackson, Christopher Rufo, Joseph Tartakovsky, and Wayne Winegarden, *No Way Home: The Crisis of Homelessness and How to Fix It with Intelligence and Humanity* Encounter Books March 16, 2021 (emphasis added).

93   "Opening Doors: federal strategic plan to prevent and end homelessness" *United States Interagency Council on Homelessness*, 2010, https://www.usich.gov/resources/uploads/asset_library/Opening%20Doors%202010%20FINAL%20FSP%20Prevent%20End%20Homeless.pdf.

94   https://entrywaytalent.org/ (accessed August 17, 2023).

95   "Zumper National Rent Report, https://www.pacificresearch.org/how-new-city-can-change-how-california-envisions-its-future-part-one/" August 1, 2023, https://www.zumper.com/blog/rental-price-data/.

96   Concerns that repealing CEQA would harm the environment are misplaced. Other states have managed to safeguard their environment without CEQA's onerous provisions that encourages abuse, stifles development, causes long delays, and imposes excessively burdensome costs. It is not beyond the abilities of California's lawmakers to adopt similar regulations.

97   See: https://dignitymoves.org/interim-supportive-housing/ (accessed August 23, 2023).

98   See: https://my.neighbor.org/our-solutions/meeting-basic-needs/ (accessed August 23, 2023).

99   https://my.neighbor.org/about-us/reports-financials/ (accessed August 23, 2023).

100   Kerry Jackson, Christopher Rufo, Joseph Tartakovsky, and Wayne Winegarden, *No Way Home: The Crisis of Homelessness and How To Fix It With Intelligence and Humanity*, (New York: Encounter Books, 2021), page 110

101 See: https://karm.org/care/ (accessed August 23, 2023).

102 "Community/Homeless Courts", https://www.courts.
ca.gov/5976.htm.

103 Mac Taylor, "California's High Housing Costs," Legislative Analyst's Office, March 17, 2015, https://lao.ca.gov/
reports/2015/finance/housing-costs/housing-costs.pdf

104 Brainy Quotes, https://www.brainyquote.com/authors/
london-breed-quotes

About the Authors

STEVEN GREENHUT is a longtime journalist who has covered California politics since 1998. He wrote this book for the San Francisco-based Pacific Research Institute, where he founded that think tank's Sacramento-based journalism center in 2009. He currently is western region director for the R Street Institute, a Washington, D.C.-based free-market think tank, and is on the editorial board of the Southern California News Group. Greenhut has worked fulltime as a columnist for the *Orange County Register* and the *San Diego Union-Tribune*. He writes weekly for *American Spectator* and *Reason* magazines. He is the editor of *Saving California,* and the author of *Winning the Water Wars, Abuse of Power* and *Plunder.* He also is author of PRI's 2022 book, *Back from Dystopia: A New Vision for Western Cities.* He lives with his wife, Donna, on an acreage outside Sacramento and has three adult daughters.

WAYNE WINEGARDEN, PH.D., is a Sr. Fellow in Business & Economics, Pacific Research Institute, as well as the Director of PRI's Center for Medical Economics and Innovation.

Dr. Winegarden's policy research explores the connection between macroeconomic policies and economic outcomes, with a focus on fiscal policy, the health care industry and the energy sector. As Director of the Center for Medical Economics and Innovation, Dr. Winegarden spearheads research and advances policies that support the continued viability and vitality of the U.S. biomedical and pharmaceutical industries to the benefit of patients and overall economic growth.

Dr. Winegarden's columns have been published in the *Wall Street Journal, Chicago Tribune, Investor's Business Daily, Forbes.com* and *USA Today.* He was previously economics faculty at Marymount University, has testified before the U.S. Congress, has been interviewed and quoted in such media as CNN and Bloomberg Radio, and is asked to present his research findings at policy conferences and meetings.

Dr. Winegarden is also the Principal of an economic advisory firm that advises clients on the economic, business and investment implications from changes in broader macroeconomic trends and government policies. Clients have included Fortune 500 companies, financial organizations, small businesses and trade associations. Previously, Dr. Winegarden worked as a business economist in Hong Kong and New York City; and a policy economist for policy and trade associations in Washington D.C. Dr. Winegarden received his B.A., M.A., and Ph.D. in Economics from George Mason University.

About Pacific Research Institute

The Pacific Research Institute (PRI) champions freedom, opportunity, and personal responsibility by advancing free-market policy solutions. It provides practical solutions for the policy issues that impact the daily lives of all Americans, and demonstrates why the free market is more effective than the government at providing the important results we all seek: good schools, quality health care, a clean environment, and a robust economy.

Founded in 1979 and based in San Francisco, PRI is a non-profit, non-partisan organization supported by private contributions. Its activities include publications, public events, media commentary, community leadership, legislative testimony, and academic outreach.

Center for Business and Economics

PRI shows how the entrepreneurial spirit—the engine of economic growth and opportunity—is stifled by onerous taxes, regulations, and lawsuits. It advances policy reforms that promote a robust economy, consumer choice, and innovation.

Center for Education

PRI works to restore to all parents the basic right to choose the best educational opportunities for their children. Through research and grassroots outreach, PRI promotes parental choice in education, high academic standards, teacher quality, charter schools, and school-finance reform.

Center for the Environment

PRI reveals the dramatic and long-term trend toward a cleaner, healthier environment. It also examines and promotes the essential ingredients for abundant resources and environmental quality: property rights, markets, local action, and private initiative.

Center for Health Care

PRI demonstrates why a single-payer Canadian model would be detrimental to the health care of all Americans. It proposes market-based reforms that would improve affordability, access, quality, and consumer choice.

Center for California Reform

The Center for California Reform seeks to reinvigorate California's entrepreneurial self-reliant traditions. It champions solutions in education, business, and the environment that work to advance prosperity and opportunity for all the state's residents.

Center for Medical Economics and Innovation

The Center for Medical Economics and Innovation aims to educate policymakers, regulators, health care professionals, the media, and the public on the critical role that new technologies play in improving health and accelerating economic growth.

Free Cities Center

The Free Cities Center cultivates innovative ideas to improve our cities and urban life based around freedom and property rights – not government.

www.ingramcontent.com/pod-product-compliance
Lightning Source LLC
Chambersburg PA
CBHW070028030426
42335CB00017B/2341